12 contemporary pieces
for PIANO

UNBEATEN TRACKS

Edited by Joanna MacGregor

FABER *ff* MUSIC

© 2005 by Faber Music Ltd
First published in 2005 by Faber Music Ltd
3 Queen Square London WC1N 3AU
Cover by Økvik Design
Music processed by MusicSet 2000
Printed in England by Caligraving Ltd
All rights reserved

ISBN 0-571-52409-5

To buy Faber Music publications or to find out about the full range of titles available
please contact your local music retailer or Faber Music sales enquiries:

Faber Music Ltd, Burnt Mill, Elizabeth Way, Harlow CM20 2HX
Tel: +44 (0)1279 82 89 82   Fax: +44 (0)1279 82 89 83
sales@fabermusic.com   fabermusic.com

PREFACE

I often think that playing the piano is like getting on a train and going on a journey – discovering new soundworlds, taking risks and being introduced to new ideas. So I asked a group of creative, talented musicians to come up with pieces that would not only stretch you technically, but would also give you other important things – a sense of groove, the chance to improvise, music that would unlock your imagination. In this book there are sad pieces, funny pieces, pieces that are jazzy, heroic or epic, poetic pieces, and pieces where you may have to stamp your foot, hum or play the mouth-organ. And of course you'll be able to perform all this music to entertain anybody you know (as well as entertaining yourself).

I hope you enjoy every bar, every riff and every tune that's been written for you here as much as I do, and happy travelling ...

Joanna MacGregor

August 2005
soundcircus.com

COMPOSER BIOPICS

All contributing composers were asked to give their own personal response to the following questions; of course, their answers can only reflect their views now and will be ever-changing:

Where do you live?
Tell us some pieces of music that have most inspired you ...
... and some individuals who have most inspired you.
Is there a story, or particular feeling behind your piece?
Give three words that best describe your music in general.
What is your favourite film and favourite book?

Each composer has also provided a performance note on
the piece contained in *Unbeaten Tracks*.

We hope you enjoy reading their answers on the next few pages ...

JOHN PARRICELLI

Where you live	North London
Inspiring pieces/individuals	Probably the music I listened to between the age of 14, when I started playing guitar, and my mid-twenties. These would include Joni Mitchell's *The Hissing of Summer Lawns*, which I still feel is a masterpiece of songcraft, in perfect harmony with sublime musicianship and production, *Bad Sneakers* by Steely Dan, *Phase Dance* by Pat Metheny, *My Song* by Keith Jarrett, *Heyoke* by Kenny Wheeler and a lot of Brazilian music, including pieces by Toninho Horta. I would say that these are also the people who have influenced me most.
Story/feeling behind piece	The feeling of the piece is melodic — and probably slightly melancholic — over a solid rhythmic base ... a combination that occurs in a lot of my music! (It's also a combination present in a lot of Brazilian music.) I do write happy tunes as well!
Three words	Melodic; straightforward; eclectic.
Favourite film; favourite book	*Cinema Paradiso* (1989, directed by Giuseppe Tornatore); *The Remains of the Day* by Kazuo Ishiguro.
Performance note	The right hand should sing out over the ostinato, which should be very steady. Bars 19—24 offer a different, more muted colour. Start to build from bar 24— bars 25 to 29 being very strong — and then gradually diminishing in intensity to the end of the piece.

TOMOKO MUKAIYAMA

Where you live	I live in Amsterdam, but was born in Japan and studied in the USA.
Inspiring pieces	Johann Sebastian Bach's Keyboard Inventions; *Grosse Fuge* for string quartet by Ludwig van Beethoven.
Inspiring individuals	There have been so many people, that it is difficult to name one ... but working creatively with other people is always inspiring.
Story/feeling behind piece	We never know which animal is stronger than the other; you should create a fantasy as to who is chasing who ...
Three words	Fun; sport; fantasy.
Favourite film; favourite book	*Gone with the wind* (1939, directed by Victor Fleming); Japanese/English dictionary.
Performance note	The left hand should be played with absolute precision while trying to give the impression of freedom in the right hand — the hands should 'play' against each other.

TOM MCDERMOTT

Where you live	New Orleans, USA.
Inspiring pieces	Fryderyk Chopin's Twenty-Four Preludes, Erroll Garner's *Concert by the Sea*, Duke Ellington's music from the 1920s, Scott Joplin's ragtime pieces.
Inspiring individuals	James Booker, Duke Ellington, Ludwig van Beethoven, Wolfgang Amadeus Mozart.
Story/feeling behind piece	There is no story but if anything, it reflects the rhythmic feel of the music by New Orleans pianist Henry Butler.
Three words	Traditional; humorous; eclectic.
Favourite film; favourite book	*Annie Hall* (1977, directed by Woody Allen); *Old Glory: a voyage down the Mississippi* by Jonathan Raban.
Performance note	*Frumba* is a highly syncopated piece in the manner of New Orleans pianists like Henry Butler and Dr John. While you often hear music that is this syncopated, it's rare that you get to see it written down: so learn it, take it slowly and gradually build up speed.

PETER SCULTHORPE

Where you live	Sydney, Australia.
Inspiring pieces	Australian indigenous chant, Gregorian chant, Indonesian gamelan music, birdsong.
Inspiring individuals	The writer, Joseph Conrad; the painter, Russell Drysdale; the architect, Andreas Palladio.
Story/feeling behind piece	Following the terrorist bombing in Bali, in October 2002, the Indonesian pianist, Ananda Sukarlan, requested pieces from composers around the world. *Little Passacaglia* is one of these pieces, and all were performed in concerts given in memory of those who died.
Three words	Straightforward; programmatic; optimistic.
Favourite film; favourite book	*The Searchers* (1956, directed by John Ford); *Lord Jim* by Joseph Conrad.
Performance note	My piece, as indicated, should be played with much tenderness: it seeks to give solace to all whose loved ones have recently died. The right-hand melody, then, should be always expressive and never obscured when it is the lower of two parts. Also, careful attention should be given to the pedalling.

STEVE LODDER

Where you live	Stoke Newington, London.
Inspiring pieces	As a classical student I digested anything by Johann Sebastian Bach, the impressionist repertoire of Claude Debussy and Maurice Ravel ... even Franz Liszt's *B minor sonata*. Later on, Herbie Hancock's *Actual Proof* was a stimulant to explore what on earth they were all up to ...
Inspiring individuals	As a jazz pianist it's impossible to escape the huge musical presence and legacy of Keith Jarrett — whether freely improvising, playing standards or experimenting with the trio.
Story/feeling behind piece	Carlos is being niggled, in danger of being severely upset ... but through a series of meditative moments manages to calm himself down, even though the irritant is somewhat persistent!
Three words	Too many chords!
Favourite film; favourite book	*Don't Look Now* (1973, directed by Nicolas Roeg); *Ulysses* by James Joyce (as a place to re-visit ...)
Performance note	Rhythmic feel is important in this piece, with a touch of latin from bar 30 onwards (the 3/4 groove) and a slightly menacing aggression to the groups in bar 7. Dynamic range is important too, in order to contrast with the *cantabile* passages. At the end, the low chords are clusters; the actual notes are not important, but keep the relative distance of hands.

KATHY HINDE

Where you live	Bristol: a city with lots happening but also quite near beautiful countryside.
Inspiring pieces/individuals	I love Bjork's music, as well as her attitude: she's not scared to stand out and be different, collaborating not only with other musicians and DJs but also visual artists. I've always been interested in Erik Satie, especially when I was learning piano, as he wrote stories alongside his music and composed pieces inspired by drawings. The work of Brian Eno is hugely inspirational, particularly a piece called *Self Storage* (created in collaboration with Laurie Anderson), in which a huge storage area was divided into smaller rooms each containing different sounds, videos and/or sculptures.
Story/feeling behind piece	I often find scientific explanations of phenomena to be quite poetic. *Meteor Shower* is an atmospheric piece that is intended to describe in music the journey of a stream of meteors entering the earth's atmosphere.
Three words	Atmospheric; textural; descriptive.
Favourite film; favourite book	*Amelie* (2001, directed by Jean-Pierre Jeunet); *New York Trilogy* by Paul Auster — the story is so intertwined and clever, it makes you want to read it again.
Performance Note	A Meteor is a particle of matter from space that enters the earth's atmosphere. Most meteors burn up in the atmosphere, leaving a streak of light behind them. When playing this piece, imagine a shower of meteors entering the earth's atmosphere and leaving beautiful streaks of light behind them, before disappearing all together.

ANDY SHEPPARD

Where you live	Bristol, although I seem to find myself more and more on the road.
Inspiring pieces	*Mother Goose Suite* by Maurice Ravel and *A Love Supreme* by John Coltrane.
Inspiring individuals	Miles Davis, Pablo Picasso.
Story/feeling behind piece	It's all in the title ...
Three words	Soft; hard; spontaneous.
Favourite film; favourite book	*Cinema Paradiso* (1989, directed by Giuseppe Tornatore); *The Kite Runner* by Khaled Hosseini.
Performance note	Many years ago when I was looking at some paintings, I realised that the canvas was a kind of window to the heart of the artist and that what was really interesting, and moving, was not just the painting itself but the feeling behind the brushstrokes. To make this piece work you have to give meaning to the inside of each note — play it with feeling and communicate this to the listener ...

PADMA NEWSOME

Where you live	Mallacoota, a remote seaside town in Victoria, Australia.
Inspiring pieces	*Fratres* by Arvo Pärt, the Adagietto from Gustav Mahler's Symphony No.5, *Tea for the Tillerman* by Cat Stevens, as well as Ludwig van Beethoven's late string quartets.
Inspiring individuals	Neil Young, Judith Glingan (my first choir leader), Erik Satie.
Story/feeling behind piece	The piece was inspired by the late-night sounds of the George Washington Bridge over the Hudson river, as heard in a friend's late summer New York apartment. The traffic from a distance sounds like the distant ocean waves, very peaceful and subtly ever-changing.
Three words	Heart; improvisation; friends.
Favourite film; favourite book	*Harold and Maude* (1971, directed by Hal Ashby); *An Imaginary Life* by David Malouf.
Performance note	All phrases are to be performed expressively and elegantly. Bring out the melodic lines, and in particular take care to perform the arpeggiated material musically and with expressive nuance.

MATTHEW HINDSON

Where you live	Sydney, Australia.
Inspiring pieces	*Pavane pour une infante défunte* by Maurice Ravel, *Vingts regards sur l'enfant Jesus* by Olivier Messiaen, *Little Passacaglia* by Peter Sculthorpe, *Ride On Time* by Black Box, *Maninya V* by Ross Edwards.
Inspiring individuals	Anyone who has the courage of their convictions and the guts to do something, not just talk about it.
Story/feeling behind piece	I wanted to write a jaunty, quirky piece in which the two hands sometimes work together, but sometimes work against each other ... a little like cogs in a machine.
Three words	Fun; extroverted; emotional.
Favourite film; favourite book	*The Sixth Sense* (1999, directed by M. Night Shyamalan); *The Bonfire of the Vanities* by Tom Wolfe.
Performance note	It is most important to try to keep a strict sense of rhythm, so that the different rhythms in the two hands really work together. Try also to make large differences between dynamics so that the overall effect is very dramatic.

JOANNA MACGREGOR

Where you live	I live right by the sea in Brighton. On one side I have a very quiet garden and on the other, lots of cafes and clubs. I can hear the sea sighing at night.
Inspiring pieces	*The Goldberg Variations* by Johann Sebastian Bach, John Coltrane's *A Love Supreme*, the music of the great Brazilian musician Egberto Gismonti and just about everything by Bjork.
Inspiring individuals	My nan — still lovely and funny in her nineties; Bob Dylan for his heroic Never Ending Tour; Martin Luther King.
Story/feeling behind piece	It's to do with driving up Highway 61, through Louisiana and Mississipi, a couple of summers ago. I wanted to write something that sounded slightly bumpy and explored the whole keyboard in a couple of pages.
Three words	Journeying; landscapes; passion.
Favourite film; favourite book	*The Night of the Hunter* (1955, directed by Charles Laughton — a scary, black-and-white fairy tale about a bad preacherman, and a brother and sister, starring Robert Mitchum and Shelley Winters); *Great Expectations* by Charles Dickens.
Performance note	I really like players who are relaxed yet alert when they play — everything they do seems natural, but powerful. Try and keep the whole of your body relaxed when you play this piece — so that moving around the keyboard, playing the glissandos and tremulos, even clicking your heel feels (and looks) easy, never tense. The left hand should have a slight kick to it; feel the shape of the chords in the right hand carefully, and sink into them. If you keep your right-hand thumb nice and loose, the crushed notes starting at the top of the second page will feel fun.

MATTHEW BOURNE

Where you live	Leeds and Manchester.
Inspiring pieces	The entire output of New York composer and saxophonist John Zorn. The work of Gerald Finzi, Frank Bridge, Kaikoshru Sorabji, Salvatore Sciarrino, Morton Feldman, Lord Buckley, Ethel Merman and Mike Osborne. Also the work of bands such as Lightning Bolt and Dillinger Escape Plan.
Inspiring individuals	My first teacher and mentor George Sidebottom, and the writer Haruki Murakami.
Story/feeling behind piece	This piece was improvised for a short film of the same name, premiered in Bristol in January 2005; its very 'Englishness' reminded me of my first music lessons and is dedicated to George, whose knowledge and wisdom has far outstretched that of any teacher I have since encountered.
Three words	Disgusting; sensual; violent.
Favourite film; favourite book	*Eraserhead* (1977, directed by David Lynch); *The Malady of Death* by Marguerite Duras.
Performance note	This piece originally started life as an improvisation and I have tried to convey its sense of indolence within this transcription. With this in mind, performers should endeavour to feel their way through the music and, in a sense, discard the rigidity of barlines and time signatures altogether ...

PETER MCGARR

Where you live	In a tiny house, on the top of a hill, on the edge of the bleak Lancashire/Yorkshire Moors (like the landscape in *Wuthering Heights*!).
Inspiring pieces	*The Walk to the Paradise Garden* by Frederick Delius, *For Emily, Whenever I May Find Her* by Paul Simon and *Missa Gloria Tibi Trinitas* by John Taverner (*c*.1490–1545).
Inspiring individuals	My late mother for her gentleness, L.S. Lowry for his perseverance, and my wife for her love and laughter.
Story/feeling behind piece	I've always thought of solo performers as part of some kind of imaginary orchestra – everything they do can be taken and used in a piece: singing, miming, imitating things ... anything! I play around with these effects, then mix them like a soundtrack to evoke the images behind the music.
Three words	Haunts; echoes; ghosts.
Favourite film; favourite book	*Whistle down the Wind* (1961, directed by Bryan Forbes) and *A very long engagement* (2004, directed by Jean-Pierre Jeunet); *Fools of Fortune* by William Trevor.
Performance note	See page 39.

8
One for Toninho*

John Parricelli

With a groove ♩ = 116 – 126

* Toninho Morta, Brazilian guitar player and composer.

© 2005 by Faber Music Ltd

cat and mouse

Tomoko Mukaiyama

12

Frumba

Tom McDermott

to Ananda Sukarlan

Little Passacaglia

Peter Sculthorpe

Sydney, June 2004

... in which Carlos avoids getting upset

Steve Lodder

* palm clusters, low down on the keyboard: left hand on white notes; right hand on black notes.

Meteor Shower

Kathy Hinde

* very delicate tone clusters at the top of the piano

tiny particles float upwards

(Ped.)→

very delicately, as if hardly

ppp

una corda al fine

anything is there . . . just open space

(Ped.)→

(Ped.)→

rit.

disappearing into nothing

(Ped.)

gradual release

On the edge of a perfect moment

Andy Sheppard

The Tides of Washington Bridge

(solo piano, no.1)

Padma Newsome

Silent Movie

Matthew Hindson

Lowside Blues

Joanna MacGregor

*   White note glissando, not fast but very smooth.
** Black note glissando, *sim.*

to George

Indians

Matthew Bourne

for Janet

Eleven nights with Glenn Gould

Peter McGarr

1. The ghosts are singing

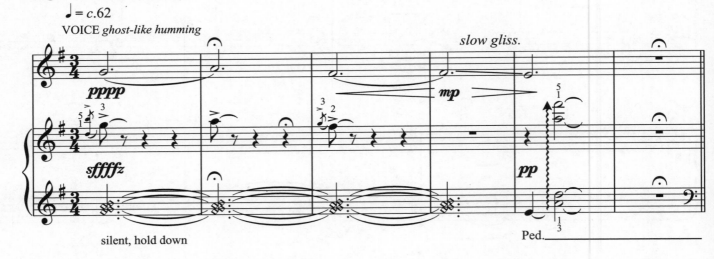

2. North-distant

*like the wind stalking across
the Northlands of Manitoba*

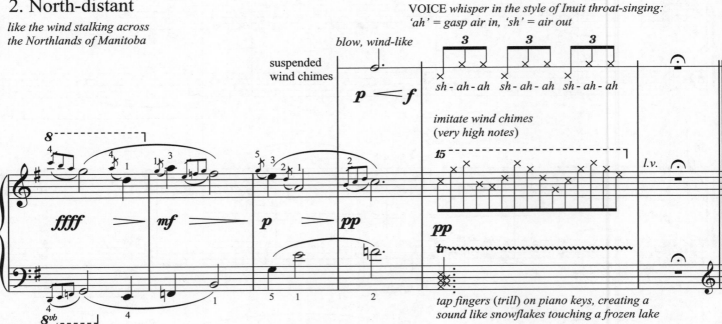

3. Snowscape

as if shivering from cold

4. Imaginary orchestras

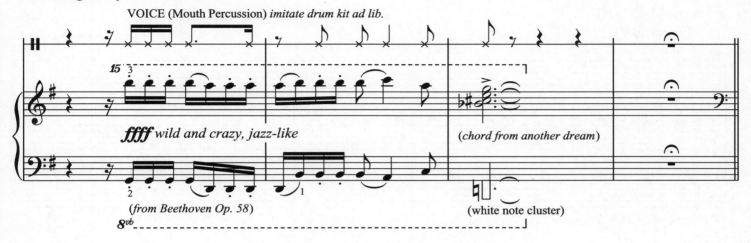

VOICE (Mouth Percussion) *imitate drum kit ad lib.*

ffff wild and crazy, jazz-like

(chord from another dream)

(from Beethoven Op. 58)

(white note cluster)

8vb

5. Hearing Mozart

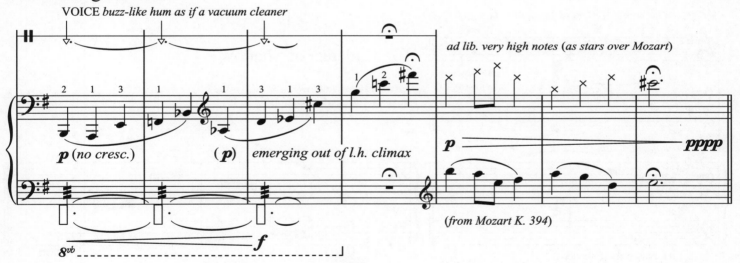

VOICE *buzz-like hum as if a vacuum cleaner*

ad lib. very high notes (as stars over Mozart)

p (no cresc.)

(p) emerging out of l.h. climax

p

pppp

(from Mozart K. 394)

8vb

f

6. Wide night

ASSISTANT with wine glass (optional)

Whistle *imitate wind whistling through telephone wires**

p

as an ancient telephone heard across the wide night plains of Saskatchewan

* if unable to whistle, blow air at given pitch

7. Sleepless in Toronto

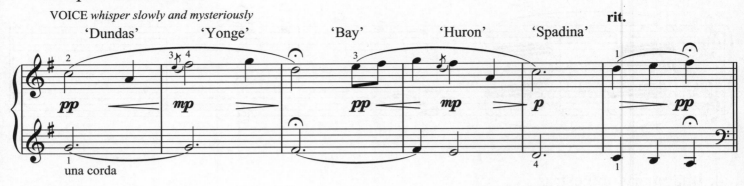

8. Aria (1955/81)

9. Homage to Orlando Gibbons

10. Cadenza of Shadow

*mime in the style of Glenn Gould
(imagine the sound, but don't play)*

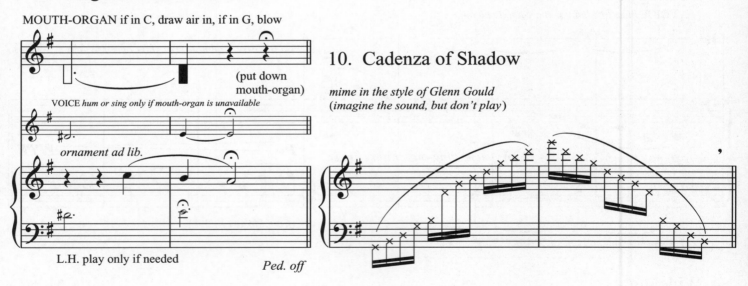

11. Pet sounds

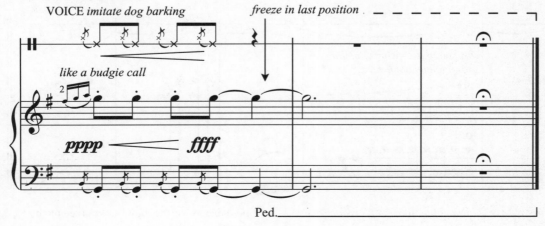

Valentine's Day, 2005
Wayne St, Openshaw.

PERFORMANCE NOTE

Eleven Nights with Glenn Gould is a set of nocturnes about the Canadian pianist, Glenn Gould, who gave up live performance when he was 31 and spent the rest of his life making recordings, radio documentaries and television programmes.

1. 'The Ghosts are singing' imagines the echoes from a deserted Eaton's Auditorium, Toronto, where Gould once played.

2. 'North-Distant': He was fascinated by the idea of Northern Canada and made a radio documentary about the train journey to Churchill, Manitoba — a place known as the Polar Bear Capital of the World.

3. 'Snowscape': There's a famous photo of Gould wandering across the snow to Caledon, Ontario. This piece evokes the scene at nightfall, when all that remains are his footprints in the snow.

4. 'Imaginary Orchestras': He's six years old. Falling asleep in the back of his parents' car, dreaming of wild orchestral sounds and he's making them all!

5. 'Hearing Mozart': He's practising Mozart. Someone turns on the vacuum cleaner. He can't hear the music. Mozart could be Schoenberg. He loves it! He discovers how his body really moves when he touches the keys.

6. 'Wide Nights': Gould spends many hours of many nights talking on the telephone. This music reflects the landscape his voice travelled across.

7. 'Sleepless in Toronto': Unable to sleep, he would drive around the streets of downtown Toronto. This nocturne is like a brief film clip — the whispered street names pass by to the piano soundtrack.

8. 'Aria (1955/81)': It was his recording of J. S. Bach's 'Goldberg Variations', at the age of 22, that established Gould as a unique interpreter. He recorded the piece again in the last year of his life, when he was 50. Here the two interpretations are stitched together to create an impression of time passing.

9. 'Homage to Orlando Gibbons': A tribute to Gould's favourite composer.

10. 'Cadenzas of Shadows': A mime show.

11. 'Pet sounds': The work closes with a bark and a birdcall. He loved animals and when he was young had many pets, including four goldfish called Bach, Beethoven, Haydn and Mozart. The last note of the piece is 'caught' and sustained by the piano pedal, like a camera catching a final fleeting image.